Change Your Thoughts.
Change Your Life.

Toolkit: 30 Day Journal

Cynthia Howard RN, CNC, PhD

Table of Contents

We become what
we think about ...

Welcome!

Change your thoughts and you change your life!

This is more than a cliché. It speaks to how we are hardwired. Study of the brain and our nervous system shows us that our thoughts emerge from our emotions which drive our experiences.

Emotions get trapped in our physical body and we can feel tired, achy, maybe have tightness in our neck or muscles, we may be impatient, irritable, fatigued. What is happening is that there are emotions that never get verbalized, instead they are expressed through our body and the daily choices we make.

And this changes how we *think* about ourselves and our world around us.

We have all had those days when nothing goes right and you get to the end of the day, tired and even confused about what you accomplished. When this becomes a theme, and every day starts off this way, it limits your progress, setting you up for more of the same.

This 30-day Journal toolkit is designed to help you learn the art of reflection so you can change this pattern, be deliberate with your thoughts, and intentional with your actions. You will breakthrough frustration and status quo thinking (nothing ever changes for me).

Learning to reflect and write out your thoughts uncovers the gold in the frustration, confusion, and the emotional quagmire. These kernels of gold are the insights and lessons, that can inform your actions and thoughts, making it better the next time.

I am so glad you are here! In my 25 years of coaching ambitious and amazing leaders and professionals, I have found writing in a journal, to be one of the power tools that provides tremendous return on the investment of time and effort.

To me, one of the biggest benefits of keeping a journal is it helps you create order when your world feels like it is going off course. Emotions may be swirling around, threatening your perspective, and this can take you off center; writing it out in a journal helps you sort through it and calm the tension and confusion. This is the first step to solving problems and expanding your perspective. By writing things out, you are in the best mindset to tackle whatever shows up.

Self-awareness is a critical characteristic for success and journaling takes you inside *you* by uncovering your fears, thoughts, and feelings.

Taking time for you is part of a self-care ritual that will ultimately help you to de-stress.

Use this toolkit to begin, or renew, your journaling practice. We have set this up as a 30-day program. This is to encourage a consistent practice of writing and reflecting to help you get the greatest value from this practice.

What is important is that you use this tool CONSISTENTLY. Daily writing, even if for 3 to 5 minutes is when you shift your mindset and your perspective. This process of reflection will retrain your brain to think through events and learn from each experience.

Enjoy this process of getting to know you!

HOW DOES JOURNALING MAKE A DIFFERENCE?

The stress reaction can be subtle with increased tension and distraction as an early signal your nervous system has begun the process of fight or flight. When in the throes of a stress reaction, your body becomes where your emotions live resulting in aches, pain, tension, tightness, restlessness and even weight gain.

Keeping a journal is a great way to unwind the stress reaction, reboot your nervous system and unlock those hidden emotions that need to be released.

Writing out your thoughts and feelings helps to:

- Reduce anxiety
- Eliminate tension
- Fight off low mood, disappointment, and despair
- Prioritize action steps
- Uncover fears so you can rationally deal with them
- Identify emotions that are hidden, but are actively skewing your confidence

Keeping a journal is very personal. We provide suggestions and want you to set it up the way that works best for you.

Let's start this process by listing any excuses you have about keeping a journal. Below, start writing out your excuses. It will help you put them behind you.!

Write out any excuses you use to keep from journaling, from not enough time to not knowing what to write. On the next page, whatever it is, put it on paper.

There is a Big Fat Elephant in the Room

We have all heard someone talk about the "elephant in the room." These "elephants" are the issues that get bigger and heavier the longer they are ignored. These elephants are costing you time, money, and opportunity. And sometimes, you do not realize they are there.

This includes the elephants that challenge a common mindset: "Stress, what stress?" or "Pressure? I can handle it. What doesn't kill you makes you stronger." And the mindset that stops all progress, "It should not be this way," and "This is the way we have always done it here."

Elephants may come in the form of distraction from what you might need, or, choices and daily behavior that sabotage your energy, focus and stamina, or a mindset of self-doubt, making it tough to accomplish what you need to get done.

Elephants are people, places, situations, past memories that keep you stuck. You may have tried to avoid dealing with them, making this elephant bigger and heavier; the only way through these is with a mindset shift. This journal program is going to do that, while helping you learn to release tension.

As an Executive Coach, I help leaders and professionals manage their mindset. Never before has mindset been so important. Here is why.

We live in a distracted world; the digital age has accelerated change and proliferated information to the point that we are drowning in it. Most of us, despite "smart phones, cars and homes," still do not manage information exposure because of the fear of missing out (FOMO). This fuels the incessant push to scroll and keep up, all while missing the moment.

I see people trying to speed up, to catch up, without realizing they are missing "the moment." A moment is 3 seconds, and this is where emotions, reactions, insights, and learning happen. This is when we appreciate people, places, and situations for what they are giving us.

It is "in the moment" when we experience satisfaction for the job we are doing or the success we have achieved.

This 30-day journaling program will help you reclaim these missed moments by learning the art of reflection.

Mindset Difference

In this toolkit we are using the 30-day card deck along with this journal and online program, to help you shift your mindset and expand your perspective to one that is energized and positive, despite what might be going on in your world.

The quality of your life is driven by the quality of your thoughts. Every moment you have a steady stream of thoughts, emotions, triggers that vie for your attention. The more distracted you are, the more likely the stress reaction is tripped, taking you further away from the thinking that will drive success.

Stress and distraction trigger the survival mode, and your thoughts become more defensive, negative, and even hostile.

This happens even if you are not aware of it! This toolkit is designed to bring your attention to your thoughts and help you control them.

Regardless of what happens "out there" in the world around us, the only thing we really have absolute control over is our reaction to whatever happens. And controlling your thoughts is the first step to a power mindset.

Thoughts are influenced by emotions and emotions are contagious. This journal gives you the opportunity to reflect and reframe your thinking and your emotions.

While you cannot control WHAT happens, you do control how you respond. Change your thoughts (and feelings) and you will change your results. Use this journal to power up an optimistic perspective that will guarantee consistent results in your life, at home and at work.

Your thinking feeds your fears or fuels your success. Use the card deck and this journal, in fifteen minutes a day, and experience the mindset difference.

Reflection

Describe a time your emotions got away from you.

Writing this out will help you recognize important details and triggers, making it easier to prevent the reaction the next time.

_____

_____

_____

FATAL EMOTIONS: DISAPPOINTMENT. DISCOURAGEMENT. DENIAL.

We have all received some type of disappointing news. Your promotion did not come through, the raise was not what you expected, you lost the bid for the job, you did not get accepted into your program—the list can go on.

Disappointment is part of living life. When you do not manage those disappointments and you become discouraged, that can be fatal. Discouragement that goes unchecked destroys self-image, confidence, and expectations for the future.

Discouragement

The dictionary definition of discouragement is "the act of making something less likely to happen." When discouragement is allowed to grow into a mood, motivation and momentum are eroded.

The erosion can be subtle. The discouragement shifts to a feeling that "things will never work out." You may try harder only to experience more disappointment, or you may give up altogether. Either way, discouragement kills drive.

This is why self-awareness is so important. You have to be able to identify your feelings and then take the right action to shift them.

6 Steps to Go from Discouraged to Determined

1. **Name it**: Whenever you feel disappointment, identify it and take action.

2. **Reframe it:** Identify three things that are going well for you.

3. **Claim it:** Engage the optimist in you and recognize that it is not permanent, and things will change. Denial is what makes this emotion fatal, capable of destroying your mojo.

4. **Talk about it:** (Or write in your journal.) Find a safe person who will simply listen. At this point, talking it out helps release the heavy emotion. You can find solutions later.

5. **Help someone else:** The tendency with discouragement is to narrow your focus and think only of your problems. Get out of yourself and reach out to someone in need.

6. **Move on:** Let it go and focus on your big vision.

In addition to these steps, do something every day to manage the stressful feelings that come up.

Denial

Denial is a defense mechanism we all use to protect ourselves from some perceived threat. Maybe there was bad news and you instinctively minimize it to get through the emergency. This temporary use of denial is helpful.

Denial becomes fatal when you use it to avoid dealing with situations that *require action*. Compulsive activity like drinking too much, overeating, shopping until credit cards max out and a number of other behaviors are fueled by denial.

These behaviors help you avoid dealing with the issues like financial strain, your bullying coworker (or spouse), signs your teenager is using drugs, dealing with your weight, feeling old, or the loss of love in your relationships, and the list could go on and on. Food, wine and other drinks, trinkets that you buy, help you compensate for your disappointments—these are all examples of denial that is fatal.

Denial happens with our own behavior and that of others. Denying your own behavior shows up in chronic blaming. If you persistently accuse others of doing something wrong, chances are the problem lies with you.

Here is an example. A client came to me distressed and ready to quit her job because her boss was blaming her for misplacing reports in the office. He was disorganized and never put anything away, so piles would grow on his desk. He would call her and accuse her of taking the document and not returning it. She did not want to talk to him about it and decided to avoid any conflict.

It is helpful to realize that in any interaction, both people are responsible for the outcome. Are you contributing to a situation by trying to avoid it?

When you avoid taking any action, you are denying your responsibility in the situation. If you feel like a victim and complain, "Things always happen to me," chances are you are using denial to avoid taking action.

Denial allows problematic situations and health risks to continue, ultimately creating more serious issues. If you have been exposed to constant pressure or traumatic events, and you are reaching exhaustion, it is time to take action. Pushing yourself beyond your ability to cope is a set up for sickness and disease.

When denial is allowed to operate without question, you turn off creativity and initiative. It takes energy to keep the truth of your situation out of your mind.

What beliefs keep you from seeing problems as they show up?

Denial is healthy when it is used in the short-term; when it becomes your 'go-to' for handling people and situations, it is destructive and can be fatal.

Suggestions to Go Beyond Denial

1. Open up to feedback. Before you shut out what someone tells you, consider this: is there any truth to what they are saying?

2. Get in touch with your fears. Does change threaten you? Afraid to succeed? What are your fears?

3. Talk to someone—counselor or coach. Your friends or family are not going to move you ahead. Talk with a professional.

4. Evaluate your life to date. Is it working out the way you expected, or has it fallen short? If so, in what way? Be objective. Have your beliefs held you back? What are they?

5. Journal every day. Writing about your experiences will help you explore your motives for making the choices you make.

Overview of the 30-Day Journaling Toolkit

This journal is set up as a 30-day program. It can also be spread out over 30 weeks, or 30 months.

Journaling is the adult's way of learning; this learning from experience comes from your reflection and being objective, as you look back at a situation. When you look back at an experience, you gain insights, and open up to potential that is often lost in mistakes, failures, emotional reactions, or, just the busyness of the day.

We live and work in the digital age where change has accelerated and there is an overload of information. The speed of change and volume of information clutters one's brain making it hard to focus on what is most important. Having a practice of writing and reflecting is one of the power tools to help you stay energized, focused, and clear.

Journaling is simple, as long as you do not overthink it. There is no wrong way to journal! This journal is set up with questions and topics for you to consider. Review the question and write out what comes to your mind. You can review what you have written, after writing for 5 minutes, to see if there is anything else you want to add.

It does not matter if you have experience journaling, there is no time like the present to start! Begin now.

Be sure go online, members.worksmart.club, and go to, *Toolkit: 30 Day Journaling Program*, where we lay out this 30 day program with instructions, audio, and additional resources that will be helpful for you as you engage in the day to day practice.

Decide if you want to schedule in time at the beginning, or the end of the day, and work through the prompt for that day. The power behind journaling comes from the consistent reflection and writing it out.

Be sure to celebrate your effort. We include the journal, the card deck, and the online program to support your transformation. We know what is possible for you when status quo thinking is disrupted. This practice will take you beyond your everyday grind.

We want you to celebrate you and your desire (and efforts) to upgrade your thinking. You were fearfully and wonderfully made and worthy of recognition.

Learning to manage your mindset is the single greatest intervention you can make, because what you think about – you will bring it about.

Did you know that any type of change is best when it happens incrementally? Celebrate your small steps!

Over the past several decades I have worked with scores of people and witnessed tremendous shifts that come from small tweaks in one's thinking.

Continue to use reflection and journaling as a strategy to power up your awareness and growth.

As a member of the Work Smart Club, you have access to the private Facebook group. Stop by and let us know what you are focused on. Share your wins and your struggles.

Everyone at the Work Smart Club wants you to know, it is an honor to walk with you and help you achieve your dreams!!

Dr. Cynthia Howard
The Work Smart Team

Write out your goal for this program.

What prompted you to take this course and what would you like to see differently in your life?

_____

_____

_____

_____

_____

_____

_____

_____

_____

TIPS TO MAKE JOURNALING WORK FOR YOU

1.Write something every day.

Setting a daily goal of writing 5 to 7 minutes can be enough to reflect and release the tensions of the day. Check out the Daily Review, online, in the module on different types of journals.

2. Keep it simple.

Carry a notebook with you at all times so when you have a thought or the impulse to write you can do so. You can use a handwritten journal, an app, or both. What works best for you?

3. Write whatever feels right.

This is for your eyes only and is not intended to be graded! Write in bullets, doodle, draw, write in a narrative or short phrase. Spell check or grammar is not important.

Write for 5 minutes and then read what you have written. Ask yourself, "What does this mean for me?" and write more as you explore what you have written.

4. Make it yours.

One of my clients likes to decorate her notebook for every theme and or season and she shares her theme with her friends on Instagram. This starts a conversation around something that is important to her.

5. Limit distractions

Make sure your environment is distraction-free. Turn off your phone, social media, and anything else that will interrupt you.

6. Count of 4 Breathing

Start the session with this technique. One of the 3x5 cards has the instructions for this breathing technique. Here it is:

1. Take a breath in, on a count of 4.

2. Hold your breath, on a count of 4.

3. Exhale on a count of 4.

4. Wait 4 seconds before breathing again.

7. Write with a pen or a finger.

You can use the computer and type or handwrite in a journal. Many prefer writing it out and find this allows for greater flow.

8. Date your entries.

Having a date on each entry helps you look back and establish a timeline of your personal growth and insights.

9. Keep your journal private.

This is important in order to feel completely free to write out your emotions.

10. Make this practice consistent.

Journaling is especially powerful when you write after difficult or happy times. You can also set up a weekly ritual to write. In order to establish a consistent habit, begin your journaling with a small increment of time, like 5 to 7 minutes, every day.

This 30-day journaling program, with the many tools and strategies, will help you unlock emotions, insights, and transform your thoughts and perspective.

And this is what will change how you show up in life.

CLEAR YOUR MIND: ATTENTION REBOOT

We live and work in a distracted world with endless interruptions and shiny objects that compete for our attention.

The Attention Reboot is a short exercise that, when practiced, will retrain your mind to focus. Learning to direct your attention is one of the most important skills you can develop!

This quick reset is the deliberate use of your attention. It is a mindfulness technique you can use to quickly reboot your focus.

<u>Instructions</u>

Let's say you are in a staff meeting. You don't like being there because it takes time away from finishing up your work. In the past, to avoid feeling the resentment, your mind wandered, and you would think about your next vacation or some place you loved visiting. Rather than being distracted by what is happening internally, you are going to reboot your attention.

To be more present, try this instead.

1. Clear your mind, take a few deep breaths.

2. Imagine this is the very first time you have been in the meeting. What do you notice?

3. Your only job is to observe. Let any thoughts drift away.

4. What do you notice? How is this different from what you normally notice?

Grab the "Attention Reboot" card and keep it with you for a day. Practice this technique throughout your day, 5-6X.

Use this technique with any person, place, or situation, telling yourself it is the very first time you have seen or heard or been there. Just observe and notice.

What is different? This ability to reboot your attention to see more around you keeps you from being complacent, distracted, smug, or stuck.

What did you notice after using the Attention Reboot?

_____

_____

_____

_____

_____

_____

_____

_____

_____

_____

_____

_____

Pull out the card, "Reboot Your Attention."

Keep this card handy to remind yourself of this simple practice.

Whenever you are starting something new, practice this at a time you are already doing something else. For example, whenever you are driving into your neighborhood, after work, clear your mind and observe, as if it were the first time!

I cannot wait to find out when you will use this technique!

REBOOT YOUR ATTENTION

Take a slow deep breath. Exhale forcefully & clear your mind.

Look around, as if it were the first time you have been there.

What do you notice. Observe.

ENERGIZE YOUR
MINDSET

30 DAY CARD DECK: USING AFFIRMATIONS

Your toolkit includes a pack of 30 (3x5) cards. The cards include affirmations and suggestions to support your effort at transforming your thoughts and attitudes.

Using positively framed affirmations is an essential element of success because, if you do not have a positive mindset, then nothing positive can happen!

The fact is *everything we think* (and feel) acts like an affirmation – it drives how we view the world. Using the affirmation cards helps you deliberately reframe your thinking.

On the cards with an affirmation, I have added "This is who I am." Using this statement at the end of the positive affirmation will help you to confirm this positive thought and defeat the nagging belief that it is not true, yet.

Much of what we believe to be true comes from early childhood. These ingrained beliefs came by witnessing, then absorbing, our parent's beliefs through their words and actions. These live in our unconscious mind and guide our perspective, choices, and actions.

Beliefs continue to live on (largely unnoticed) until they are challenged. When life presents options and experiences that challenge your beliefs, you might feel resistance, fear, anger, or distaste against the challenging belief.

This is what happens in the "mid-life" crisis, after a divorce, loss of job, and any other life event that seriously challenges one's deeply held beliefs about how life is "supposed" to turn out.

My own experience with challenging beliefs came fairly early in my career when I was laid off from my job. I always believed nursing was "safe" from the types of restructuring so prevalent in other industries. I struggled with "who I was," without my job title. I started my own business out of necessity, and even though I replaced my salary within 6 months, I did not see myself as a successful entrepreneur until years later.

I went through this again when my husband was in the final inning of his life due to unforeseen health complications. Once again, my "status" was changing from married to single despite a vision of living out our years together.

Here is another example of one of my clients, who we will call Deidre. She struggled with moving ahead in her field. She had the education and experience but lived with an uneasy feeling that she was not ready. Even though, from the outside everything said she had what it took, these "feelings" kept her from taking the risk and applying for promotions.

Working through this stuck place, we uncovered an old belief of her father that she had internalized. When Deidre was a little girl, he had attempted a business venture and he failed. This put their family through a period of financial hardship and left her father with a sense of uneasiness and self-doubt. Without realizing it, he passed this along to his daughter with his frequent warning, *"you can never be too sure."*

Deidre used journaling to explore her feelings of uneasiness, and then supported her newly empowered self with an affirmation, "I believe in myself. I am confident. That is who I am."

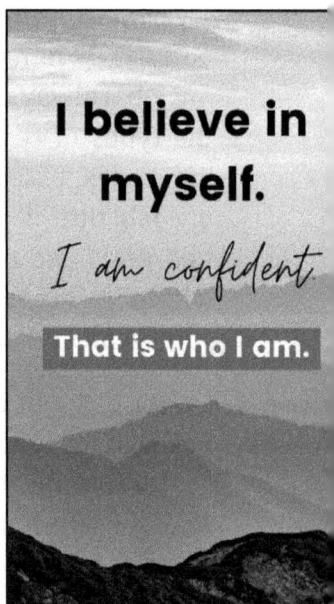

I believe in myself.

I am confident.

That is who I am.

On the next page, take a moment and write out your experience of resisting change when life challenges your deeply held beliefs.

Are you resisting any changes that life is requiring of you?

Write about an experience that is challenging the way you think "should" be happening.

_____

_____

_____

_____

_____

_____

_____

_____

_____

_____

Tips for Coloring

As children we had coloring books, crayons and chalk and would draw, doodle and color as part of play. Then and now, coloring is a great way to de-stress, relax your mind and release the tension and negativity of the day.

Researchers have found after coloring for 20 minutes, participants reported feeling more energized, content, and mindful. Mindfulness is when you are fully present and open. This is what helps you reach, what I call, your *Impact Zone*.

Your Impact Zone is that space where your mind is calm, and you feel energized. This is when you are clear and focused and have access to the best part of your brain, to make decisions and take in information.

We are living and working in the digital age where distraction is the new normal and information overload has bloated our brains. This creates brain fog and compromises focus. And the more this happens, irritability increases.

Use the coloring book and journal to release tension, anxiety and increase your ability to be mindful. The long-term benefits include greater satisfaction, concentration, and creativity.

1. Feel free to skip around in the journal.

2. Set your timer and color and or journal for twenty uninterrupted minutes. This will build your focus and concentration.

3. Do not be afraid to feel. Your emotions are your lifeline to your energy and creativity. Let tears flow, anger bubble up and sadness come forward, all to be released. Leave whatever comes up in the journal – walk away refreshed.

4. Use coloring pencils, crayons, felt tip, watercolor and anything that strikes your fancy.

On the next page, and throughout the book, are black and white images. Color the designs, as you wish, and allow your mind to release and relax as you do.

Keep yourself open, there is no judgment on the design, coloring is simply a way to release the tension and the clutter in your mind, as you let go of any lingering emotion that gets in your way of showing up at your best.

Color. Doodle. Using short phrases, write out what you are feeling, in the margins.

Using the Essential Oil of Lavender

The essential oil of lavender is obtained from an evergreen, woody shrub with violet blue flowers found all over the world. France is at the center of the many growing regions. To get 1 pound of oil, you need 170-250 pounds of plants. We provide a therapeutic quality of lavender essential oil from France.

It is the most popular of the essential oils; it gets its name from the Latin word, "lavare" meaning "to wash" or "to bathe." It was discovered while a French chemist and founder of Aromatherapy, R.M. Gattefosse was working in the lab. He burned his hand and wanting to dull the pain, he instinctively stuck his hand in a glass beaker filled with lavender oil. He was shocked at how quickly it healed.

Decades later, it is now a powerful remedy with many uses around the house.

In addition to being safe for adults and children and helpful for treating skin conditions, the essential oil of lavender can also balance one's mood, rejuvenate and soothe a tired attitude and help to slow down someone who is stuck in the hectic pace of busy-ness.

I invite you to use the essential oil of lavender to balance your mind and body. This is one of the amazing properties of this essential oil, while drugs either stimulate or sedate a person, lavender is able to do what is needed and restore homeostasis – the body's natural state of balance.

I have included lavender in this kit because using essential oils is a natural safe way to balance your mind and emotions. Lavender is an amazing oil. It has a harmonizing effect on the nervous system, the emotions, and the physical body.

Helpful with:

- Relief of muscle aches
- Stress relief
- Menstrual pain (blend with carrier oil and massage over abdomen or use in hot compress)
- Colds, flu, asthma (apply to your chest)
- Insect bites, burns (apply directly to the skin)
- Insomnia

Lavender supports and soothes our "life force" (of the heart) and is calming of the spirit, relieving irritability, reducing palpitations, and lowering blood pressure.

It blends well with all oils and has no precautions. It can be used directly on the skin and with children.

For more on essential oils, take our course, *Everyday Essential Oils*, in the Work Smart Club.

How Do Essential Oils Work?

Essential oils work in a variety of ways. One is through their absorption in the body via the skin. It takes about 20 minutes for the oil to travel through the body's blood stream and reach the nervous system.

How you apply the oils depends on the intended purpose of the oil. For example, lavender is known to relieve muscle tension, heal damaged skin, and also minimize cramps. In these cases, it is best applying the oil directly to the abdomen and massaging into the skin.

Essential oils are also absorbed directly into the blood stream via inhalation, crossing the blood brain barrier, impacting the nervous system within minutes.

Research in olfactory perception (inhalation) has shown that it only takes a few molecules to have a significant effect on the central nervous system. Think about a time when you were immediately transported back to a memory after smelling someone's perfume, the aroma of coffee, freshly mown grass, cookies baking, and any number of aromas.

Researchers are discovering that odors can and do influence mood, evoke emotions, counteract stress, and even reduce high blood pressure.

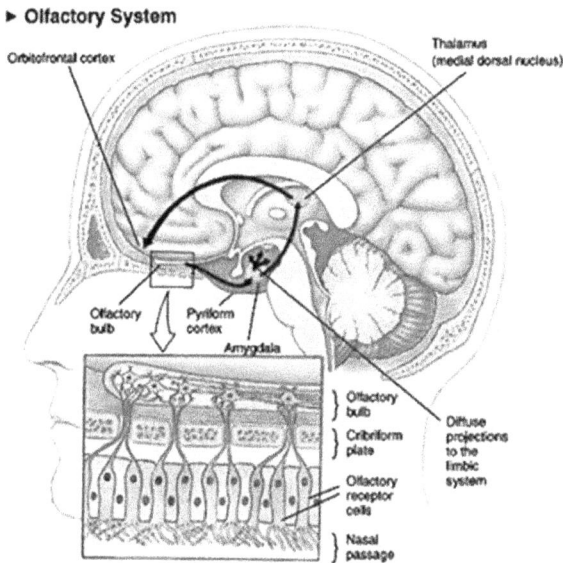

Figure 1 Olfactory Bulb (inset)

It has only been in the last 20 years that research into the olfactory system has begun to reveal the mysteries of how aromas are processed and interpreted by the body.

Smell is the only sense in which the receptor nerve endings are in direct contact with the outside world. The olfactory bulb does not require the thinking brain (cortex) to process the information. Olfactory nerve cells are also the only nerve cells that repair themselves if damaged.

Smell begins in the nasal cavity and proceeds to the olfactory bulb where "messages" are initially processed. This message is transported to higher centers of the olfactory system where perception and memory is triggered. The second target is the emotional center of the brain (the limbic system) where emotions and emotional memories are triggered.

How to Use the Essential Oil of Lavender

1. Inhale directly from the bottle.

2. Put a few drops of lavender on a cotton ball and put inside your pillowcase.

3. Add a drop to tea, hot or cold, and ingest.

4. Add 2-3 drops to the palms of your hand, then rub your hands together, and cupping your hands under your nose, inhale deeply.

5. Visit the online portal and download the pdf with many more practical uses for your lavender oil.

6. Natural skin care and exfoliation treatment. In a small bowl, add small about of water or chamomile tea to 2 tablespoons of finely ground oatmeal, to form a smooth paste. Add 3 drops the essential oil of Lavender. Apply the paste to your face, neck and décolleté, massaging in small circles. Leave on for 2 minutes, then wash off. Your skin will feel refreshed as you will from the aroma!

Stop by the Facebook group and let us know your favorite use of lavender!

DAY 1

TYPICAL DAY

In detail, describe your day, from the time you wake up and then go to bed.

As you look at your day, what could you do differently tomorrow?

_____

_____

_____

_____

_____

_____

_____

_____

What will you commit to doing differently?

_____

_____

_____

_____

_____

_____

Relax. Release Tension. Color

DAY 2

IDEAL DAY

Write out what your ideal day looks like.

Compare this to your typical day, on Day 1, what needs to change?

Day 3

EXPECTATIONS

What do you **EXPECT** to happen in your life?

Are you thinking ordinary, same old, same old, or are you expecting something bad to happen, or something wonderful?

Think about your expectations for love, life, work, and success. Answer the following, choose all those that apply!

I expect to

- ☐ Achieve my goals, no matter what.
- ☐ To screw it up.
- ☐ To struggle. Life is hard.
- ☐ To be in debt for the rest of my life.
- ☐ To experience tremendous opportunity. I am ready.

Write out your expectations:

_____

_____

_____

_____

_____

_____

_____

_____

Expectations are an important part of the "success" mindset. The dictionary definition of expectation is "an event likely to happen." Expectations can be expressed directly, "I am expecting to win," and indirectly, "nothing works out for me."

Expectations provide the clues to underlying emotions. In the Mindset Difference section, I talked about how feelings are the driving force (energy) behind our thoughts and the choices we make. Even if your thoughts are positive and you tend to worry, rehash old resentments or quarrels, think about the negativity of the past, these underlying feelings become your expectations.

We know a lot more today about how our brain operates. It turns out our brain is plastic; this means you are capable of learning, well into our later years.

And what this plasticity also implies, is when the default mode is negative, this becomes the first thought and your attitude. Likewise, if your think positive or see opportunity, this becomes your first thought.

This happens because more than learning, our brain likes to conserve fuel, so it defaults to the feelings and attitude most often used.

Day 4

CHANGE YOUR FOCUS

Based on what you wrote in Day 3, if you are focused on something bad, or rehash what has already happened, would you like to release those thoughts and emotions?

This question is hinting at whether you are *ready* to let go and give up a habit of mind. We are hardwired to protect ourselves from emotions that threaten our continuity.

What this means is that if you are used to thinking "catastrophe," or worst-case scenario, in order to be prepared for the worst, you end up believing this is what you can expect.

On the other hand, if you are confident in your ability to handle whatever comes up, you are going to expect the best, because you have a habit of seeing yourself succeeding.

Look at the following list and rank each of the fears, with 1 being the biggest fear and 6, the least.

- ☐ Being rejected
- ☐ Missing out
- ☐ Losing money
- ☐ Losing friends

☐ Looking foolish
☐ Not being loved

Write about a time when you experienced one of the fears:

_____

_____

_____

_____

_____

_____

_____

_____

_____

Looking back, did that experience change how you viewed yourself? In what way? Write about that.

_____

_____

_____

Day 5

COLOR

Color outside the design ... live outside expectations.

DAY 6

FEARS

Are you held back by fear? What are you _not doing_ that you really want to do?

Write out those activities and or risks you avoid.

Day 7

COMFORT ZONE

Write down everything you want to try out. Where do the activities fall in the chart below?

Naming your desired activities makes them more approachable. Use the next page and write them out.

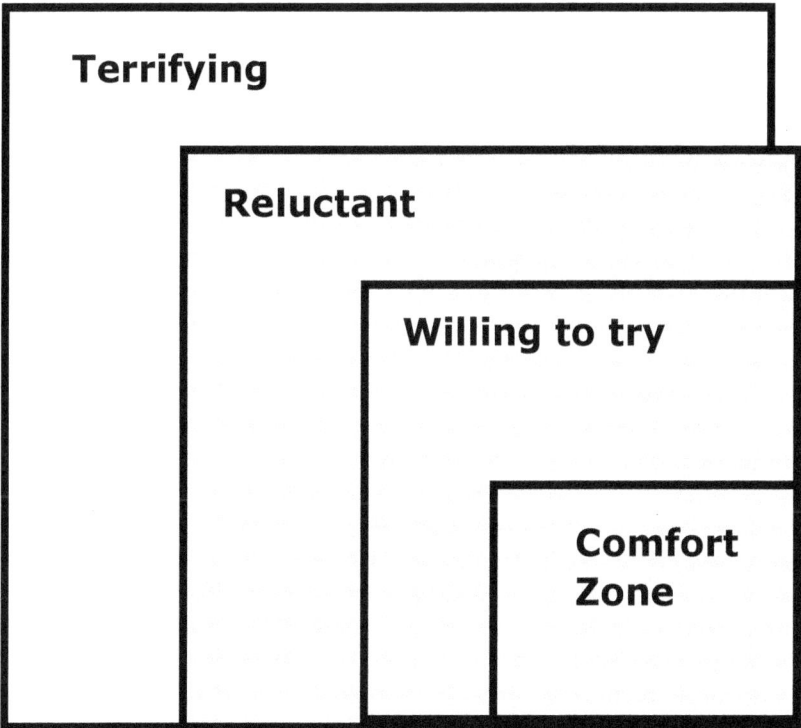

Terrifying

Reluctant

Willing to try

Comfort Zone

Terrifying:

_____

_____

_____

_____

Reluctant:

_____

_____

_____

_____

Willing to try:

_____

_____

_____

_____

_____

_____

Day 8

EXCUSE ZONE

What are the excuses you give to yourself to keep from stepping out of your comfort zone?

No need to judge yourself, just write them out.

When you face these excuses or fears, you diminish their power. Write it out:

DAY 9

SELF-DOUBT

How do you experience self-doubt? Write about a recent experience:

_____

_____

_____

_____

_____

_____

Day 10

COLOR

Let go of any frustration or other emotions that drain you ... let it go as you color.

DAY 11

BODY SCAN

This is a good practice to refresh your awareness.

It is amazingly simple. Throughout the day, stop what you are doing and scan your body from the top of your head to the soles of your feet. Give yourself 5-6 minutes for the entire process. The scan takes about 15 seconds, the writing and reflection takes a few minutes.

Notice any aches, tension, tightness, any emotions, thoughts, you name it.

Now, jot down what you noticed. No judgement: simply write out exactly what you noticed.

When I scanned my body, I noticed:

After you have finished writing, start with the first thing you wrote down. Let's say, you wrote, "Tight neck."

Have a conversation with the "Tight neck," and ask it what it wants you to know.

Go online to the audio, Body Scan, part 2, and listen to that, then write out exactly what comes up.

For example, the "Tight neck," may be a reference to the "pain in the neck" client you dealt with, or a boss, etc. Use the audio to relax your mind and open up to the flow of your consciousness.

Recharge...

DAY 12

YOUR THOUGHTS

You are where you are today because of your thoughts yesterday.

Today I thought:

_____

_____

_____

_____

_____

Where do you want to be? How might your thoughts be getting in the way?

Do not be afraid to stand out. Go for it!

DAY 13

MINDFUL EXERCISE

Every moment is about three seconds. The practice of mindfulness is to be fully present in each moment.

Grab the "Mindful Exercise" card and practice this for a few days. Follow the prompts on the card.

Write out what that experience was like. What did you notice as you become more present and mindful?

_____

_____

_____

_____

_____

_____

_____

Think about your day, when does your mind wander? In meetings, when eating, during what activities, or with whom?

Write out your observations:

_____

_____

_____

_____

_____

_____

There is no time for cut and dried monotony.

There is time for work.

There is time for love.

That leaves no other time.

- Coco Chanel

Color the labyrinth and release the negativity, clutter, and noise in your mind.

DAY 14

GRATITUDE

Gratitude unhooks your brain from the stress reaction.

Start a list of everything you appreciate and are grateful. Come back and add to this list. Review when you are in a slump and want to be encouraged.

DAY 15

COLOR

As you color, bring up feelings of appreciation and gratitude, flood your being as you think about people and or situations for which you are grateful.

Day 16

FACE YOUR ELEPHANTS!

Elephants are those issues that bigger and heavier when you ignore them.

Take a moment and write out those things that you have put off dealing with because of time, and a host of other excuses. Putting them on paper will help you face them. It diminishes their power.

Maybe you drink wine every night after work, even though it makes you sluggish in the morning. Do you snack when no one is around, sabotaging your healthy eating plan? Are you afraid to speak in public? Have you wanted to go for that promotion but lack the confidence?

Whatever it is – make a list of your "elephants."

What excuses do you tell yourself for not facing these issues? Write them out.

Day 17

PICK AN ELEPHANT

Choose one elephant you want to confront. Name it and write out your plan to break through the status quo.

Live YOUR life.
There is no
do-over.

Day 18

COLOR

Relax as you color. Let your thoughts drift...

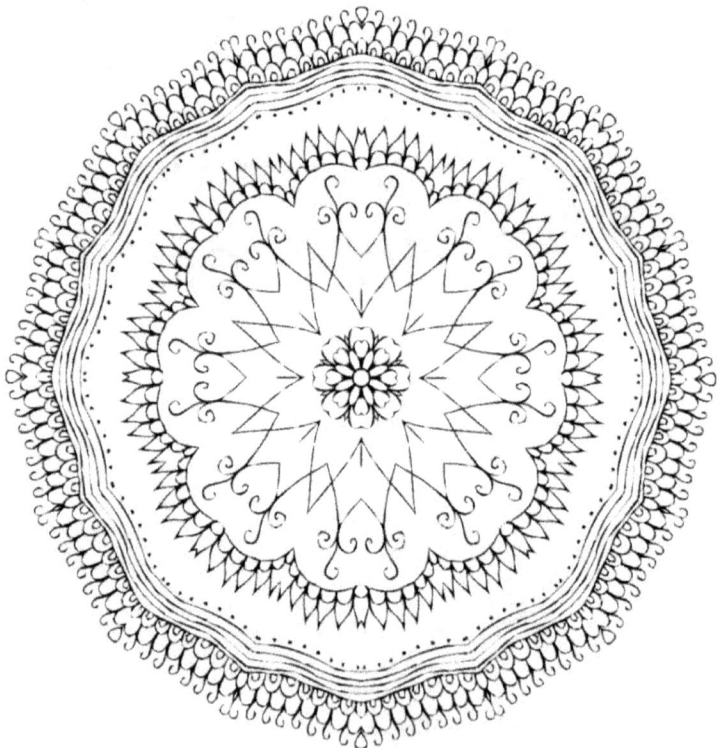

The worst enemy to creativity is self-doubt.

- Sylvia Plath

Day 19

EVERYTHING YOU LOVE

Make a list of everything you love:

1.

2.

3.

4.

5.

6.

7.

8.

9.

10.

11.

12.

13.

14.

15.

16.

17.

18.

19.

20.

21.

22.

23.

24.

25.

26.

27.

28.

Day 20

GRATITUDE BREATHING

Looking at your list from yesterday, think of these things an
allow the feeling of love to expand in your chest, feel
throughout your entire body.

BREATHE in appreciation.

BREATHE out frustration.

Practice this for 60 seconds.

Notice how you feel afterward?

Select those that apply:

- ❑ Relaxed in the chest area
- ❑ More expansive
- ❑ Fresh perspective
- ❑ More energized
- ❑ Forgiving
- ❑ Content
- ❑ Grateful
- ❑
- ❑
- ❑
- ❑
- ❑

DAY 21

COLOR

As you color let your mind drift... focus on the color and the shading ... release any worry, tension, or emotion.

Day 22

SAY YES

Today I said YES! to:

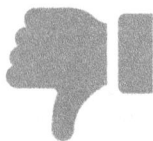

_____

_____

_____

_____

_____

What do I need to say NO to, and do more of what I want?

_____

_____

_____

_____

_____

Reflect on your ability to be assertive. What gets in the way?

Day 23

SUCCESS LOG

Keeping a log of your successes can be extremely helpful. By making this a habit, you learn to focus on those things you do well. Like many people, who experience self-doubt from time to time, when you are in a confidence crisis, you can return to this list and refresh your mind (and your confidence) with your accomplishments.

Keep your list open and add to it weekly. This is your running list of all the things, in which you have been successful.

Successes include simple things, like walking around your neighborhood, drinking your water goal for the day, making your lunch, losing 2 pounds, or something more complicated at work like hitting a deadline or benchmark. These are your accomplishments, not your children or those at work.

Open your mind to your accomplishments and write out whatever comes up. Tomorrow, next week when you think of something, come back, and put it on this list.

On the next page, do a brain dump and write out everything that comes up.

1.	1.
2.	2.
3.	3.
4.	4.
5.	5.
6.	6.
7.	7.
8.	8.
9.	9.
10.	10.
11.	11.
12.	12.
13.	13.
14.	14.
15.	15.
16.	16.
17.	17.
18.	18.
19.	19.
20.	20.
21.	21.
22.	22.
23.	23.
24.	24.
25.	25.

Day 24

CELEBRATE

Do you reward yourself? Think about your recent successes, or milestones you have achieved.

Now plan a celebration to acknowledge your hard work:

_____

_____

_____

_____

_____

Day 25

COLOR

Creativity comes from your love of life. Love is the emotion of creation. Love is the magnet for all good things. Color. Allow the feelings of love to fill you...

Day 26

STRENGTHS

Do you think about what you are good at, or what you need to work on?

Having a strengths focus will quickly move you ahead because you will be more energized and motivated during difficult times. Your "strengths" are those things you are naturally good at, you enjoy it, and when engaged you do not feel like you are working, even though you may be making an effort.

Weaknesses are those things that drain your energy and when you engage in them you struggle and do not show up at your best.

Areas that need improvement are not always weaknesses; these are areas you may need some skill development or more experience, in order to develop a proficiency.

Most people think, "But wait, I need to focus on my weaknesses to get better at ..." What ends up happening with this approach is people end up with really strong weaknesses, and by focusing on their failures, success is elusive.

Research has found that people are more successful when they lead through their strengths.

Learning to operate from your strengths does take a mindset shift. I hope you will go through this exercise and identify those things you do really well. Because many people (and organizations) focus on their weaknesses, people do not learn to distinguish between their skills, talents, and their strengths. In fact, many spend most of their working life doing something they are good at but that does not energize them.

Is this true for you? Are you drained by your daily work? When you think about your work, are you using your strengths or operating from skills you learned and developed to "get the job"?

Discover Your Strengths: Answer the following questions:

What did you like to do as a child that you still enjoy doing?

Are there things you have picked up quickly?

Where does your attention naturally go?

What energizes you when you are engaged in that activity?

_____

_____

_____

_____

What makes you feel like the "real" you when engaged in it?

_____

_____

_____

_____

_____

What motivates you? What do you do because you love to do it?

_____

_____

_____

_____

_____

Example of Using a Strength to Balance a Weakness

Here is an example of how to use one's strengths to support a weakness. Debbi loves coaching her staff and finds it easy to handle conflict and bring people together. She finds it challenging and draining to analyze problems.

If she wanted to "work on" her weakness, it is best done by focusing on her strengths which includes bringing the best out of people. She might decide to hold a brainstorming session to "collect data" on the problem, and then have a round table discussion about the problems. She could delegate the measurement aspect of the problem-solving process to one of her staff who excels in collecting the numbers and displaying them in graphs and spreadsheet.

In this way, she utilizes her strengths in bringing people together while engaging with her team highlighting their strengths.

Identifying your innate strengths will allow you to flourish. Operating from your strengths literally magnetizes your performance and increases your satisfaction—even when things get tough.

Day 27

COLOR

DAY 28

MISTAKES & FAILURE

If you are *not* failing from time to time. You are playing it too safe.

What chances have you taken recently and failed at? Write this out...

_____

_____

_____

_____

_____

_____

_____

_____

_____

_____

_____

What do you tell yourself about taking risks and making mistakes? This may be similar to what you heard from your parents growing up. Write this out.

_____

_____

_____

Day 29

COLOR

DAY 30

REFLECTION

Think about the last 30 days. What stands out?

In the last 30 days, I noticed:

_____

What will you do differently in the next 30 days?

Next Steps

After using this journal and the card deck, what are 3 things you want to change in your daily activities?

Daily Changes

What needs to change in your daily activity?

1.

2.

3.

Daily Keeps

What will you continue to do that is working?

1.

2.

3.

Types of Journals

The following are suggestions for journals. I routinely use a small 5x7 size notebook to carry with me as an idea journal. Use one or all of these at different times to capture inspiration.

1. Idea Journal

Carry a notebook with you and jot down any ideas you have for a book, poem, fashion design, or any other creative pursuit that interests you. This may be a thought you have to explore later.

This journal is helpful when you have initiated a new project and you continue to think about it. Write down your thoughts as they come up and free your mind!

2. Work Journal

Keep a notebook in the breakroom of your job and have staff write down things they are grateful for, acts of kindness, and observations they have. This can be related to Six Sigma projects, special initiatives, or a general practice. Review at a staff meeting or during a special meeting to discuss "Matters of the Heart" or the "Breakroom Conversation."

3. Memory Book

Start a journal for your child, niece, or even a friend's baby and periodically write down what is happening, adding pictures and memorabilia. Have entries on the child's birthday, your birthday, and other special dates. Give it to the child on his or her sixth, tenth, or sixteenth birthday.

4. Couple or Family Journal

Keep a journal in the kitchen and use this to communicate in happy times and especially during conflict. This can be used to focus on gratitude and family values and also to reflect on the growth years.

5. Reflection Journal

Use a journal to reflect on major events, difficult experience, both work and personal. Reflection increases self-confidence, builds skills, strengthens strategic thinking and develops your interpersonal skills.

DAILY REVIEW

Just like the name suggests, this daily ritual provides a quick overview of your day.

In 5-7 minutes, at the end of the day, reflect on, and write out the answers to these 3 questions:

1. What worked?

2. What did not?

3. What is next?

Keeping this journal, every day, offers a record of the strategies and tactics that help you accomplish your goals.

Visit the online portal for more on this type of journal. We also have the templates available for download.

Once you do a daily review, do a weekly review every Friday, and a monthly review giving you a record of your progress over the course of a year.

This is powerful for both personal and professional applications.

Message from Dr. Cynthia Howard

Thank you for your purchase of the Journal Program! We are one of your biggest fans and want you to succeed!

We are committed to helping those leaders and professionals who want to move further ahead than they thought possible.

Now that you have this resource, you are part of the Club, your center for Work and Well-being.

Our mission is to transform the workplace through inspired and innovative leadership; we help you succeed and together, we achieve an amazing goal.

We love to know how this resource impacted you and what we can do to improve, I want to hear from you. Please tell us what you think:

- What insights did you get from this resource?
- Will you be changing how you do something? If so, in what way?
- Would you recommend this resource to others?

- Was something confusing or lacking in this resource?

Please email me at contact@worksmart.club.

Stay energized!

Dr. Cynthia Howard

Dr. Cynthia Howard

CEO, Chief Energy Officer, Work Smart Consulting

Founder, Work Smart Club

www.worksmart.club

About the Work Smart Club

The club is an online space where you learn, grow, and develop your leadership skills and build an authentic leadership brand. The journey to success requires a strategy and support. We help you with both.

www.worksmartclubmembership.com

We provide an online platform of courses, live events, virtual coaching, and webinars. We know the pressure leaders face in driving results and achieving their goals. Our resources are available 24/7 and will help you stand out.

worksmart
thinkdifferent

Impact Zone

Have you ever thought, "I need more impact as a leader!" We understand the struggles leaders have sandwiched between administration and the front lines, with competing demands.

To support leaders' ability to make a bold impact, we have put together a 6-month leadership mastermind.

We want leaders to ignite their passion and unlock their potential in a leadership mastermind.

What is a leadership mastermind?

Professional Development with Expert Support

A mastermind is a group of highly motivated individuals, committed to growing personally and professionally. The small group meets monthly and is focused on leveraging the power of this single purpose—to foster personal and professional success, drive results, and unlock potential through coaching, support, and accountability.

This is facilitated by Executive Coach, Dr. Cynthia Howard.

www.worksmartthinkdifferent.com

Cynthia Howard RN, CNC, PhD

Pioneer of the resilient mindset · Performance Expert · Executive Coach · Black Belt Lean Six Sigma

Dr. Howard works with individuals and organizations to breakthrough complacency and disrupt the status quo. Using an innovative approach to leadership development, we unleash potential in your leaders.

www.worksmartthinkdifferent.com

Let's connect:

Facebook: @worksmartcoaching

Twitter: @drcynthiahoward

Linked in: @drcynthiahoward

Pinterest: @worksmartclub